BETTA FISH

THE SIMPLE GUIDE TO CARING FOR YOUR MAGICAL BETTA

WALTER JAMES

Please consult a licensed professional before attempting any techniques outlined in this book.

By reading this document, the reader agrees that under no circumstances is the author responsible for any losses, direct or indirect, which are incurred as a result of the use of information contained within this document, including, but not limited to, — errors, omissions, or inaccuracies.

www.publishing.admore-marketing.com

CONTENTS

FOREWORD

There is something truly magical about the fish-keeping hobby.

... But besides looking nice, does caring for fish actually add to your life?

It absolutely does! Fish tanks have so many benefits for those who own and interact with them. Studies have shown that owning fish has positive physiological and psychological effects. Having a fish tank improves your mood and reduces stress and anxiety. Observing fish elegantly float around their homes for just a view minutes lowers your heart rate and blood pressure.

There are many benefits to owning fish beyond this, and bettas specifically are awesome fish roommates to have. With all these advantages, however, comes some responsibility. Fish help us in so many ways (half of which we don't realize immediately), so it is essential that we return the favor with our care for them. This book covers everything you will need to properly care for betta fish. This way your little guy or girl will live a very long, happy, and healthy life.

Lets get started...

To you it's just a fish, but to me it is a
cute little person with fins!

-Unknown-

INTRODUCTION TO BETTAS

"Betta Splendens" (or Siamese Fighting Fish)

This is the formal name of the gorgeous and very popular fish in the aquarium hobby. It's easy to see why bettas are so popular... They have bright colors and shades that captivate viewers. They are fresh water fish, which makes finding a proper tank and care a simpler process. Their long fins float elegantly and effortlessly in the water. They have unique personalities and react to their owners and visitors of a tank. Also, they are relatively durable and do not require a lot of maintenance.

The Betta Splendens you can find in almost every pet

store today differ greatly from what the breed originated from almost 200 years ago. This book will mainly
cover Betta Splendens, but there are actually many
other betta species. As of 2017 there are around 73
species classified under the genus (A biological classifi-
cation of living and fossil organisms) *Betta*. All
betta are considered small but they vary greatly in
several features, including size and colors. While all
these bettas are all incredibly beautiful and great
aquarium species in their own right, none are as
prolific as the Betta Splendens. Their demand has
allowed them to become the best known of the species
and it is common for them to simply be referred to as
bettas.

This book covers all aspects of these magical guys and
girls. We will look at the history of bettas along with a
small, more precise look at the different species. After
this look in the past and the development of the beautiful species, all "care" aspects will be covered. Bettas are
often described as being "no maintenance" fish that
can be kept in small bowls. This is very misleading
information. They are some of the easiest fish to
keep however they still require basic, proper care. You
will learn about everything from proper "housing" to
feeding. Unfortunately, just as all of us do, Bettas can
get sick. Common problems and diseases are covered
along with the best ways to treat them. All kinds of tips

and tricks are sprinkled throughout the book, so if you are a novice or are an experienced Betta hobbyist, I promise it will be a worthwhile read.

If you are lucky enough to own one of these fiery fish, you will discover that with proper care they are very active and entertaining. They are quite intelligent as far as fish go, as they can even learn tricks. It is not a stretch to say that a betta can really become a part of your family.

Let's get started by having a look at their history...

Getting through life is simple... Just add a BETTA!

-Unknown-

HISTORY

In order to understand how the colorful bettas we see today came about, we must travel back to Southeast Asia in the 1800s. More specifically, head to the river basins of the Mekong and Chao Phraya Rivers which run through Thailand, Cambodia, and Vietnam. There, in small peaceful streams, rice paddies, drainage ditches, and even little puddles are where Betta originally come from.

Image of the Mekong River which has an estimated length of 3,703 miles (4,350 km). It runs through Vietnam, Cambodia, Thailand, Laos, Myanmar, and China. Image Source: L joo (public domain work - Creative Commons license)

They looked completely different from what you picture when you hear "betta". Back then, they had a plain dull olive green or brown color which allowed them to camouflage in the still, warm waters. They also had short fins that didn't draw much attention. Bettas were a very common fish during that time as they were very durable. They could live through rough conditions and survive dry seasons in water with very low oxygen content. We will look more into how betta are able to survive these conditions in Chapter 3.

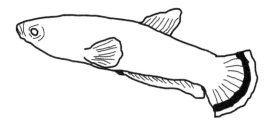

Wild bettas look like the little guy in the image above. Very different from the betta you have swimming in your tank, right?

Seeing as they were such a common fish, they became intertwined with the culture of the region. The people of Thailand referred to them as *"Pla Kat"*. Pla Kat loosely translated means tearing or biting fish. They earned this nickname as they are highly territorial. Male Bettas are especially bold as they will look to guard their nests and territories against any and all threats.

Siamese Fighting Fish

Although bettas hotheaded temperament has made it possible for them to survive for centuries, unfortunately, it also allowed for a more dark side of their history to take place. People would collect bettas and conduct fish fights. Huge bets were placed on fights between two males. Gladiator like battles would be organized, as the dark tradition grew from a small village activity to a large spectacle. It is said that people would lose money, property, and even family members in bets. The fish suffered the most, however. Fights would be stopped before one of the fish would die, but the loser (sometimes even the "winner") would be severely injured and torn up. This means they would often die not long after a fight as they could not recover.

In the wild it was common for betta males to attack one another, however, in those cases the loser would quickly leave the more dominant males territory. Both fish would be fine and continue with their day. In these organized fights betta males were forced to continue fighting as they were in a tightly confined space.

"The Jewel of the Orient"

As individuals looked to gain an advantage in the practice, breeders began popping up. Although the bettas we know today grew out of a dark organized fighting practice, the breeding of them allowed for some positive effects. People began to appreciate bettas not only for their fighting spirit but instead for their beauty.

When fisherman would pull up their nets, at times there would be a brightly colored, shiny betta fish stuck in the nets. This was seen as a good luck charm. The fisherman would keep the fish in a bowl and take care of it. This appreciation of the fish has allowed for bettas to become what they are today. Over the years, breeders took different beautiful elements from these fish and created what we commonly see in stores today... Betta Splendens.

Unfortunately, the fish fighting traditions are still secretly present today in parts of the world. It can be noted however, that most of the world does not tolerate any animal fighting for sport. In the countries where bettas originated, the law does not take the tradition lightly. Fish fighting is now a serious offense punishable with jail time.

Bettas Today

Bettas have come a long way from their past in Southeast Asia to becoming one of the most popular aquarium pets of the Western world. They brighten up aquariums with their impressive colors and personalities. "*Aquariumists*" have learned how to take proper care of these magical guys and girls, and now bettas can live great lives with their owners. *You are also well on your way with this book*. Owners have been able to teach them tricks and even despite their aggressiveness, have successfully cohabitated bettas with other fish and even other betta. To find out more about how you can potentially get started with this, turn to Chapter 8: Compatibility.

It is great to get a full understanding of where Betta come from. It makes it easier to see why it is important for them to be in a certain water temperature, or why there should be a good amount of plants in the tank. Don't worry if everything I just mentioned doesn't make sense just yet. We will cover all aspects of betta care later on, but for now, let's take a more in-depth look at the different varieties of bettas...

BETTA *then the rest!*

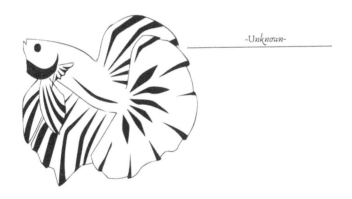

-Unknown-

3

SPECIES/BREEDS

B etta are always seen as gorgeous, but simple aquarium fish. There is a lot of miseducation when it comes to the species. Because of their wide popularity and availability in stores, people are often shocked when they find out there are actually over 70 different species of bettas. Fish enthusiasts aren't able to ignore many of the other betta species, however. They make great aquarium subjects and also display beautiful traits, even though they may be more subtle ones. Because of their more subtle look, most shops don't have other betta species readily available.

In this chapter we will look at 5 of the more popular betta species and observe different details surrounding a betta fish. This includes their size, anatomy, and the unique way they breathe.

. . .

5 Betta Species

This list is not organized in any particular order (i.e. best to worst). They are simply some of the more popular bettas enthusiasts enjoy having.

Emerald Betta (Betta Smaragdina) 50-60mm / 1¾–2"

Emerald Bettas earned their nickname by having a shiny green sheen on their body and fins.

Physical Appearance:

- Both males and females have a short fins and feature a round tail.
- They have a bright green color with black webbing on their scales.
- They can also feature some reddish touches either on their fins or bodies.

Origin: Nong Khai, Thailand

Mouthbrooding Betta (Betta Pugnax) 60-70mm / 2-2¾"

Mouth-brooding Betta and other bettas feature an up-turned mouth. This makes them top feeders. They spend their time patiently hiding, and then when something floats by at the surface that looks appealing they quickly come up, grab it, and head back down to cover. Male mouth-brooding bettas also carry their babies (eggs) in their mouth until they are ready to hatch.

Physical Appearance:

- They have some of the smallest fins of the species.
- They have a round tail and pointy fins (the tail can be somewhat pointy as well at times).
- Their colors vary, as they can be anywhere from an orange color to a gray or even feature green/blue spots.

Origin: Penang, Malaysia

Peaceful Betta (Betta Imbellis) 50-60mm / 1¾–2"

Peaceful Betta are, as their name suggests... peaceful. They can easily be kept in community tanks as long as they are with other peaceful species, and the tank is of appropriate size with enough hiding spots.

Physical Appearance:

- They have a round tail with a dark body.
- They have bright blue or green markings on their bodies that contrast beautifully against their dark background.
- Their dorsal fins are a mostly blue-green color and the ends of their tail and fins are bright red.

Origin: Spread throughout Thailand, Malaysia, and northern Sumatra.

Slender Betta (Betta Bellica) 80-90mm / 3-3¾"

Slender Betta are a slim and longer species of betta.

Physical Appearance:

- They feature short fins and a spade-shaped tail.
- A female has dark dots on her fins and tail
- A male is more intensely colored and has green highlights.

Origin: Pengkalan-Pegou, Malaysia

Siamese Fighting Fish (Betta Splendens) 60-70mm / 2-2¾"

Hands down, Splendens are the most popular betta. They come in a variety of colors, shapes, and fin shapes. The extensive breeding of Betta Splendens has allowed for them to develop unique fin shapes and colors.

Physical Appearance:

- Great variety of colors.
- Fins with different shapes ranging from round, to split, to heart, and more.

Origin: Menam River, Thailand. Has been introduced to several countries even outside of Southeast Asia. Because of fish farm escapes, populations have been established in Brazil, Colombia, and the Dominican Republic.

Betta Details

It may seem like an exaggeration, however, knowing specific details about bettas including anatomy, origin, and breed details will help you become a better caretaker. Gaining this knowledge will allow you to provide a great life for your fish pets. It is a sad sight, walking into pet sections of stores and seeing hundreds of betta stored into small cups, closely packed up next to one another. Although they are "surviving" many are suffering in the conditions they are in. Only when you learn more about how the breed actually lives comfortably, can you understand how much stress they are under.

Anatomy

At first glance, male and female bettas share many of the same anatomical features. Male bettas generally have a much flashier look and are larger than their female counterparts. Their bodies have a cylindrical form which tapers off to meet their "tail" fins (Caudal Fin). Betta have fish scales, which can be compared to armor which helps protect their soft internal organs. Healthy bettas will display beautiful scales and colors on their body. If they are stressed or sick, you will notice their coloring is a lot duller and they can display dark horizontal lines along their body.

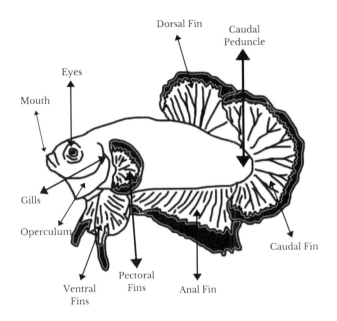

Mouth:

Betta fish have quite the grumpy-looking face. This is because they have an upturned mouth that helps them suck in air and feed up at the surface. It also allows them to make bubble nests, which is how their offspring are able to be fertilized.

Here is something truly unexpected... betta fish have greater jaw strength than that of great white sharks. Yup, you read that right. The betta you have swimming in your tank, has a more powerful jaw than a great white (*by size proportion). Don't worry though, although they have a lower jaw full of tiny sharp teeth, they cannot harm humans.

Betta are carnivores, and in the wild they feed on different insects, larvae, and scraps larger animals leave behind. Their teeth assist in the breaking down of food before ingestion.

Eyes:

Betta fish have 2 protruding eyes on each side of their head. They cannot blink and on close inspection you will notice their iris (center of the eye) is black. Bettas have very good eyesight, as they are able to recognize their owners and can get agitated by their own reflections in a tank.

Dorsal Fin:

Fins play an important role in keeping fish balanced and stabilized in water. This is no different with betta fish. Their dorsal fin is located on top of their bodies and can vary in shape and size depending on what type of betta it is. Just as with sharks and dolphins, betta use their dorsal fin to travel in a straight line.

. . .

Caudal Peduncle:

The caudal peduncle refers to the thinnest section of a bettas body that connects to the caudal fin. It is simply the connection between tail fin and body.

Caudal Fin (Tail Fin):

The caudal fin is what propels a betta fish forward. Extensive breeding of betta has allowed for the creation of a great variety of fin sizes, shapes, and colors. We will take a more detailed look at some of the more common tail types bettas have been bred to have later on in this chapter.

While the intense breeding of bettas has allowed for many magnificent tail fins to develop, it made them very different from their wild counterparts. Bettas bred to have long flowing tails are actually quite poor swimmers. Their fins are too long for their bodies and this makes them very easy prey in the wild. They are, however, gorgeous to observe in an aquarium.

Anal Fin:

The anal fin is located underneath a bettas body. This

is another fin that is perfectly positioned to help stabilize our fish in the water. Just as a boat uses a "keel" under its "body" or hull for stabilization, bettas have this naturally on their bodies.

Ventral Fins:

The ventral fins are often also referred to as the pelvic fins. They can be quite long and thin depending on the type of betta and are located just below and behind the gills. The ventral fins of a male are much larger than those of a female.

These fins assist bettas in turning and stopping.

Pectoral Fins:

These are the last 2 of the 7 fins bettas have. These fins are constantly in motion, helping guide a betta through the water. They can vary in size and color depending on the species of betta. Some owners refer to these fins as betta ears because of their flappy, ear-like appearance. They of course do not help bettas hear anything.

Operculum:

The operculum is a shield that covers a bettas gills. It's

job is simple, to protect a fish's gills. While both male and female bettas have this protective shield, males have an extra membrane underneath there as well. This membrane is often referred to as a "beard" and allows us to more easily distinguish between a male and a female.

When betta want to look more intimidating, or when males show off a dominating dance, they flare up their entire bodies. This includes the operculum and, of course their beards.

Gills:

Betta have gills, which allows them to extract oxygen from water. This is one way that allows bettas to live and thrive, however, amazingly bettas can also thrive in low oxygenated water environments. Theirs gills alone would not allow them to survive in these conditions. Let's see how they breathe in more detail below.

Breathing

Betta fish are definitely unique when it comes to their personalities and looks, but they also breathe in a very special way. As mentioned before, one way bettas breathe is how all fish breathe, with their gills. In simplest terms, fish will suck in water through their gills. As the water transfers through, the interior walls of the gills will absorb and remove the dissolved oxygen in the water. Oxygen is then transferred into the bloodstream and able to spread throughout the body. This is an amazing process that allows fish to live and thrive underwater.

Moving waters, like that in rivers and oceans will constantly pick up oxygen from the air. This is great for fish as it's how they breathe. In small, stagnant, warm waters, however, much of the oxygen will seep out. These conditions are lethal to most fish, but bettas can thrive in these environments. *How come?*

If you already own a betta, you may have noticed that they sometimes come up to the surface for a bite of what appears to be nothing. You didn't put any food in the tank, so what are they up there for? Well, it turns out that bettas can breathe directly from the surface of the water. They have something called a *labyrinth organ*. This organ allows them to transfer oxygen from their mouths into a format that their gills can process. A betta will grab some air with their mouth, pass it over the labyrinth organ, push it out through their gills, and this way transfer the oxygen into their bloodstream.

Having these two methods of breathing has allowed

bettas to survive in small ditches, rice paddies, and puddles. It is important to realize that this is an adaptation for survival. Bettas can technically **survive** for a long time in a body of water only the size of wine glass. This, however, does not mean they **thrive** and flourish in these poor conditions. Their adaptation allowed them to survive temporary conditions like a dry season. Some experts, or betta breeders state, it is perfectly fine to keep a betta in glass or a cup, but this is incorrect. These should only be temporary environments. We will look at proper housing conditions in Chapter 6.

A betta in your tank will still do most of it's breathing under water. However, if the tank has lower levels of oxygen, or if it feels like it, it will come up for a bite of fresh air.

Betta Variety (Tails, Colors, and Patterns)

Due to breeding, betta fish have developed a wide variety of different fins, colors, and patterns. There is so much variety in shape, size, and color that it can all be quite overwhelming, even for the experts. I break it all down below to make it as simple as possible.

Tails:

There is great variety in the fins and tails of bettas nowadays. They can be long and flowing, fan-like, spiky looking, and even short and sturdy. Below is a list of the main tail and fin types of bettas.

Combtail

The comb-tail got its name due the comb like appearance of the caudal fin. The tail fin on a comb-tail has a fanlike shape with rays that extend beyond the fin webbing. This gives the fish a spiky and spectacular look, especially while flaring. Because of the fins large size compared to the rest of the body, the tail can have a droop to it.

Crowntail

This tail has a very similar look to that of a comb-tail only that it features less webbing and more of the extended rays. The tail has a very spiky appearance, and it is a tail type that is very easy to recognize.

Delta/Super Delta

A betta with a delta tail starts narrow at the body and then widens, giving it a triangular shape. The name originates from the Greek alphabet. Delta signifies the letter D which is drawn or written as a triangle, hence the name delta.

The difference between a regular delta and a super delta is simply the extension of the tail spread. A super delta tail gets close to a 180 degree spread. A full 180 degree spread would be considered a *half-moon* tail, which is listed further down below.

Double Tail

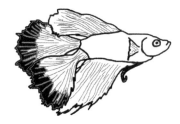

This one is very straightforward... a double tail simply signifies a double caudal fin.

Half Moon

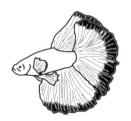

A half moon tail is very similar to a *super delta* tail only that it reaches a full 180 degree spread. Bettas featuring a half moon are shaped... like a half moon, or capital D. This shape is highly sought after as it looks spectacular in a tank. It is important to note, however, that fins this large are very unnatural. Half moon Betta are poor swimmers and carrying all that fin can get them into trouble that can lead to tail damage.

Round/Fan Tail

A round tail is also very straightforward... This simply means the caudal fin is round in shape. It is sometimes referred to as the fan-tail, as it resembles a fan.

Spade Tail

The spade tail is very similar to the round tail. The main difference is that rather than the tip of the tail being round it ends at a point. The tail resembles the shape of a spade in a card deck.

Plakat

This is a short tailed betta fish. It is named plakat as it resembles closely to wild bettas. These are stronger swimmers as they have natural, smaller fins.

. . .

Rosetail

Rose-tail bettas have a similar look to *half moon* bettas. They both have caudal fins of 180 degrees or more, just that rose-tails feature more branching. It is said that this effect looks similar to that of ruffled rose petals, hence the name... rose-tail.

Veil Tail

This is the most common tail available in most stores. A veil tail betta has a long flowing tail similar to a...

well... veil. The fins of a veil tail betta are usually long and hang.

Colors

The colors of a betta have greatly evolved past the dull colors they originally sported in Southeast Asia. Normally a darker greenish or grayish color to assist hiding in still, murky waters has now become an array of different vibrant pigments. Betta fish colors today are not as simple as yellows or blues. Read on below to learn more about some common colors of this exotic fish.

Black

Black is a very unique color in betta. There are 3 types of black, all with different levels of pigmentation. The black colors are *melano, black lace,* and *metallic black.* Melano black is the darkest of the bunch. It is a very sought after color as Melano females are infertile, this makes it a rare specimen. Black lace and metallic black bettas can also feature a deep black color but nothing like the melano. These species are more readily available as they can be bred more easily.

.　.　.

Albino

Albino bettas have no pigmentation and so are solid white. Just as most albino animals, this betta will have pink or red eyes. Unfortunately, these fish usually suffer from very poor eyesight and can go blind quickly. They are very rare.

It is also possible to have a completely white betta fish that are not albinos. We can differentiate the two colors by looking at their eyes. White bettas will have black eyes.

Blues & Greens

Bettas can be many different shades of blue. From a bright "Royal Blue" to a "Steel Blue", so many blues have been developed. Even the very difficult color to determine, *Turquoise* is available. This is a mixture of blue and green that feels as though it can change color depending on the light.

Green by itself is difficult to find in bettas but possible. Dark green is one of the more sought after colors, as it is one that is typically rare.

Orange

Orange bettas are typically on either the extreme bright side of the spectrum, or on the paler end. It is common for them to have brighter spots of orange on both the body and fins.

Purple

This is a truly spectacular color in the world of bettas. It is hard to find a completely purple betta, as they commonly have some blue or copper touches to them.

Red

Red is a common color seen in bettas. Although it is very common, it is still a color and stands out in a tank.

Patterns on Betta

It is also very common to distinguish bettas by the patterns on their body. These patterns are named after how many colors are on a bettas body, how they are patterned, and where they are from. As you may have noticed by now, there are endless possibilities when it comes to finding a unique betta. Let's continue with most common patterns below...

. . .

Solid

This is a very straightforward pattern to determine in bettas. This simply means that the betta is a single, solid color, throughout it's fins and body. A deep red is the most common solid color.

Mask

Bettas typically have a different colored head than the rest of their bodies. It is normal for it to be a shade darker and then the body has the brighter pigmentation.

A mask pattern is unique, not because the head is a different from the body, but because it is the same. It's as if a betta is wearing a *mask* to blend in with the rest of their body. The fins can be different colors, but everything from the head to the caudal peduncle will have the same color.

Bi-colored

A bi-colored betta implies that the fish has two colors. The body will have one solid color and the fins will have another. Highly contrasting colors are what's mostly sought after. *The head of the betta can be darker and the fish will still be considered a bi-colored betta.

Cambodian

The Cambodian betta pattern is a slight modification of the bi-colored pattern. The Cambodian pattern always sports a white or off-white to pink body color. This is then contrasted with brightly colored fins, which are usually red.

Butterfly

Butterfly patterns are very similar to bi-colored patterns. The difference is that around half of the fish's fins are the same color as the body. Almost 50% of the fins will have the same color as the body and the remaining 50% of the fins will have a pale or see through look to them.

Dragon

The dragon pattern displays a betta body that has thick, white, and metallic looking scales. The fins can be any color, however, they are usually red.

· · ·

Marble

The marble pattern in bettas got its name from the patterns in marble. Marble betta feature random splashes of somewhat line-like coloring all over their body. The patterns are usually brightly colored on a light backdrop on the body.

What is amazing about bettas with this pattern, is that it can change as they age. The splashes of color will change places, or will show in a different form.

Multicolored

A multicolored pattern simply features a betta that has three or more colors.

Life is good, BETTAS make it better!

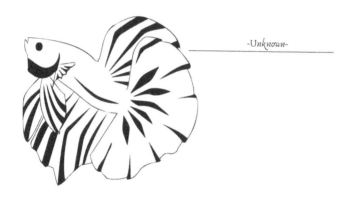

-Unknown-

4

CHARACTERISTICS

Now that we have learned about the history of bettas and how to identify them, we can look a bit more into some of their unique characteristics. These elegant little fish have very special personalities. They can be friendly and curious, or stubborn and hide at the sight of any movement outside of their aquarium. It's all about getting to know your betta and observing their likes and dislikes. This graceful species is truly an awesome pet.

Flaring

Flaring is a spectacular show a betta will put on when it wants to show dominance. Male bettas are typically the ones to display this behavior. They will make themselves appear as big as possible, by straightening out all of their fins and opening up their gill plates. It is meant to intimidate or impress, and it definitely gets the job done.

A bettas long fins usually have a droopy appearance to them and they are generally quite small fish. So when those long fins unfurl, their body inflates, gills flare, and their color looks to get brighter the message definitely come across.

So why might a betta do this?

There are a number of reasons but the most common one is intimidation. They want to show other fish that they are the dominant ones and that this is their territory. If it has tank mates, your betta is demonstrating that it is guarding its territory and the tank may be too full. If the betta is in a tank by itself, it may have seen its own reflection in the aquarium's glass. This can be enough to spark their primal temper, and so attempt to demonstrate dominance.

Another reason bettas can flare is if they are stressed. Conditions in their tank may not be suitable and this is how they voice the stress of that. It could be that water conditions are unsuitable, or they are feeling sick.

When they are sick they can alternate between highly aggressive and passive.

Lastly, if bettas are excited or ready for breeding, they can flare. A male will flare at a female who will then display submissive posture. This behavior should not last long however, as they need to be in good condition to breed. There are some rare cases of bettas flaring every time they are fed. It is not common for this to occur but it is a possibility. In general, flaring puts a lot of stress on a betta, and can cause illnesses. Although it is natural for them to display, it is not something that should be seen a lot, as it usually means something is wrong. A flare is great to see here and there, but shouldn't be a constant state.

Whoever said that dogs were man's
best friend... never owned a BETTA!

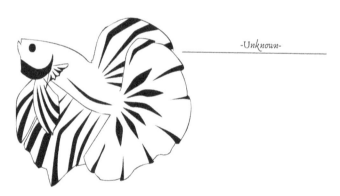

-Unknown-

5

PICKING A BETTA

Now that you know all about the different betta species and all the magical colors and patterns that are available, it's time to find one to purchase or adopt. Just as with all popular pets, there are some breeding methods that are not organized in a way that's best for the animals themselves. This makes the process of picking a new betta a tad more difficult. You want to *save* the betta that are being bred and living in poor conditions and provide a more positive environment for them. However, by doing this you may actually help these unethical breeders as you are supporting their business. I find it best to do some research before purchasing. Visit some of your local stores and look at the living conditions of the fish. Don't be afraid to ask questions to employees and see if the staff is knowledgeable. You will be able to identify quickly if the place you are considering purchasing from actually cares about the wellbeing of their fish and animals.

Let's explore some great places to find a betta...

Local Stores & Big Box Stores

In your local area there can definitely be some great businesses that sell betta fish. It's great to build a relationship with these places. You will be able to tell quickly that the fish are being raised in great conditions and that they are experts in the field. As you gain experience and knowledge in the hobby, it's great to meet with other passionate people. They will give you tips should something go wrong and best of all, help you make additions to your "fish family". If there is a specific fish you are interested in purchasing, they can help make it happen.

Online

Thanks to the internet, even if you live in a secluded, remote area that doesn't have any stores that sell fish, you can purchase a betta. Online you can connect with like-minded betta hobbyists and safely purchase one of these magical guys or gals. Many stores also have the option to purchase online and it is likely that they will ship to where you live. The betta will be labeled appropriately and packaged very carefully. This way they are handled with care as they make their way to your home.

As you are researching online, you may also come across some betta experts that blog about their experiences. They make videos and online content about how to best care for bettas and other tips and tricks. They provide excellent advice and sometimes they also breed their own bettas. You can then support them by purchasing from them and if you follow them online, you can be sure that the fish are raised in outstanding conditions.

I always recommend checking reviews when purchasing online. Websites like eBay have a great system that allows you to see how a seller is rated.

Health Is Key

I recommend for people purchasing their first betta to find one that is as active and healthy as possible. Some more experienced hobbyists try to find sick bettas to help and heal them. This is definitely for the more seasoned "aquariumists" as it requires medications and almost constant care. I suggest those starting out to get a lively betta that "speaks to you" so to say.

How can you tell this?

You can tell that a betta is healthy by observing their body and behavior. Their body should have healthy coloring and not appear to be fading. Also, their stomach should not appear to be bloated or abnormally large. This could mean that the shop is over feeding or that the betta is suffering from an illness.

After making sure that their body looks good and healthy, have a good look at all of his or her fins. They shouldn't be damaged or clamped together, but rather flowing elegantly in the water. If the fins look clamped, the betta may be sick or highly stressed.

Behavior like flaring at you, building a bubble nest, and quick movements as you observe it, are all great signs of good health. I think it is best to follow your gut and simply purchase the fish you feel best about. Many times fish are not in optimal conditions before we purchase them. When they are moved into an appropriately sized tank in your house, they heal up and potentially show a whole new side of their bubbly personality.

You may have a very specific betta in mind that you want to purchase. Like a *Cambodian-Butterfly* for example. In this situation you may have to get in touch with a breeder online and work out a purchase with them. If you are more open to what kind of betta you would like, then simply trust your instincts and look for a healthy betta that speaks to you. It is pretty much impossible to make a wrong choice with these amazing little fish.

Once you have your betta, you can begin acclimating him or her to their new tank at home... this is not as simple as emptying their cup in a tank. Let's explore the process in the next chapter, "Housing a Betta".

To most, I am no one special, but to
my BETTA, I rule the world!

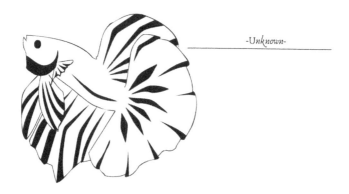

-Unknown-

6

HOUSING A BETTA

Housing is one the most critical aspects of taking care of a betta. The tank is literally where he or she will spend mostly **all** of their time. So it is crucial that it is set up in a way that allows them to live their best fish life. I recommend having proper housing set up before bringing home a new betta. This way you can be sure that you have all the proper equipment and you won't harm the fish as you rush out to get any forgotten items.

Aquarium

The first item on your shopping list should be an aquarium. This brings up one of the most highly debated and controversial topics in the betta community.

What size tank does a betta need?

Some enthusiasts claim that since bettas have a history of surviving in puddles, that they can live comfortably in a tank that size of a wine glass. As I mentioned before, they only survived in these conditions during droughts and it was not the norm. Also, why would you want your beloved fish to live its life under these circumstances?

Most of the tanks you see marketed towards housing a betta are terrible options. They are much too small and the pre-existing decor they contain can be harmful to their fragile fins. I find the absolute bare minimum size tank for a betta is one that holds 2.5 gallons (9.5L) of water. The more optimal choice is a tank that holds 5 gallons (19L) or more. This may sound like a large tank for one small fish, but it cannot be understated that they absolutely need the space.

A tank of that size won't break the bank, and it will help keep your betta happy and healthy for as long as possible. Very determined betta owners may be able to get away with a 2.5 gallon tank, but it will take more frequent water changes and conditioning. Decor will also need to be expertly planned out to provide proper housing. Generally, a 5 gallon tank or larger is the most suitable option.

Cycling

"Cycling" a tank describes the process of forming friendly bacterial colonies in a new tank. This allows the fish to have a healthy environment to live in, without high levels of toxic ammonia and nitrates. The process can take some weeks to complete, so be patient to be sure that your betta enters the correct environment.

Cycling requires you to add pure ammonia or fish food to a tank. The bacteria will feed on this ammonia and the natural "cycling" process will begin. Depending on your location, certain tap waters will contain enough compounds for your tank to naturally undergo the cycling process. I recommend for you to test your water so you can see if your water is properly conditioned to house a betta. A completely cycled tank will have measures of 0 ammonia, 0 nitrite, and around 5 nitrate. You can easily pick up some items from your local pet shop to help jumpstart the cycling process. Follow the instructions on the back of products and speak to a shop assistant.

.   .   .

Everything Else

So what else will you need?

When getting a betta, our aim is to replicate optimal conditions they would have in the wild for them inside their aquarium. To best do this, we need to remember where they originally come from. In Southeast Asia they lived in still, warm waters, with plenty of foliage or places for them to hide.

Warm Water

Betta fish thrive in water temperatures between 76-82°F (24-27°C). This means that depending on where you live, you may need to purchase a water heater. I recommend at least getting a thermostat so you can properly monitor the temperature for your fish roommate. If you live in an area that is cold or has cold winters, a water heater is definitely something to consider for the wellbeing of your fish. An alternative may be to place your aquarium in a room that remains at a consistent temperature, or close to a radiator (not too close). Keep an eye on the thermostat, so you can be sure the tank remains in the right temperature range.

. . .

Tranquil Water

A filtration system is very helpful to have when you own a betta. It helps keep the water clear of debris, and toxic buildup. It is possible to keep a betta without a filter, but this requires you to perform a water change almost every other day. Yes, every... other... day! Not only is this a lot of work for you, but this routine of being captured every other day for a water change can be traumatizing for your betta. Purchasing a filter is definitely a worthwhile investment. I recommend getting an adjustable sponge filter. They are relatively cheap and as they are adjustable, make them a perfect solution for bettas. Betta need calm waters with no strong current, so a filter will need to have a "low flow" option. Their typically long fins don't make them the best swimmers. Bettas look their best and feel happiest when the water is still, warm and peaceful.

Decor

A lot of the decor possibilities in your bettas tank come down to your own personal preferences, however, there are some things to keep in mind. Betta fish have fragile fins, and they can be quite clumsy swimmers. It is best to get decor that has no sharp edges, hard plastic materials, or holes where they can get trapped in. Fake plants can be a great option, as they don't require a lot of care. It is best to get to get *silk* fake plants, as they are soft and cannot hurt your betta. A setup that contains both some plants that root at the bottom of the tank and some that float on the water's surface is optimal. Your betta will have plenty of places to hide and rest towards the top and bottom of their home.

Live plants are a great option to add to your bettas tank. They are beautiful additions, and bettas love to lounge on the leaves and hide in them. Plants also help keep the water clean and with excellent oxygen levels. If you do decide to get live plants, it is important to also purchase an appropriate lighting system. Plants need specific lights to grow and continue to live. Without good lighting for the plants, the tank can become rotten and toxic fast.

With live plants will also come a need for substrate. Substrate is the material (sand, gravel, etc.) that sits at the bottom of a tank. Not only does it create a better looking scene in a tank, it is also practical. It helps filter water, and it traps waste and debris from freely flowing around. Bettas do not have a preferred substrate as they rarely hang out at the bottom of their tanks. They don't burrow or bottom feed as some other fish do. The most important thing to keep in mind is to have the substrate be a smooth material. I will continue to repeat it, these little guys and girls are fragile and easily find their way into all sorts of trouble. Sharp rocks won't be a good solution.

One important addition, that is often overlooked, is a lid for the tank. Bettas are great jumpers, as they were sometimes required to jump from one puddle to the next for survival. Although it is not something you will see often, it is still something to be prepared for. Some kind of cover is great to have, or you will need to lower the water level in the tank.

Prepare The Water

You will not need to purchase any special water for your betta's tank. Tap water is fine to use, and you will only need to add some water conditioner or a de-chlorinator. Standard tap water usually contains some chlorine and other properties that can harm bettas. Adding some water conditioner (by products specifications) will be enough of a treatment to the water.

Some beginners have asked me if bottled water is a good water source for their tanks. It may sound like a great idea, but bottled water doesn't have many of the minerals that are great for fish. Simple tap water is the best solution, it turns out to be a lot healthier for your betta, and cheaper for you.

If your tank has a lid, it is fine to fill it up to almost maximum capacity. If you do not have a lid yet, remember that bettas are prone to jumping. Without a lid, I recommend not filling up the tank past 80% of its capacity. This way, you won't risk your new roomie accidentally hopping out of the house.

Adding a betta to its tank

Moving homes can be a stressful experience, and it's no different for a betta. He or she will need to get *acclimated* before entering their new residence. This simply means that the temperature of the water they are currently in, will need to match the temperature of their new tank. This is a very important step, as just dumping your betta in a new tank can shock the poor guy or gal.

When you get your betta in a cup or bag, you can begin acclimating it by simply "*floating*" the cup or bag in their new aquarium. After 15 to 20 minutes the temperatures will match and your betta won't experience an intense shock. Also, never add the store water your betta was in into the new aquarium. This old water can transfer infections and diseases to it's new environment. It is best to net them out of the old water, and then very gently place them into their new home.

. . .

Cleaning & Water Changes

If you have a filter in your tank, cleaning and changing water won't be a lot of work. You will only need to change around 20% of the water every week. This number changes depending on the size of your tank. The smaller the tank the more water you should change.

Depending on how thoroughly you want to clean the tank, you can decide to leave your betta in the water as you perform a water change, or you can remove it. I recommend performing a more thorough cleaning every month or two, and then smaller water changes every week.

It can be helpful to get some test strips which will help evaluate water quality. This will allow you to know exactly when you will need to perform water changes. You can test the water weekly and then decide if a water change is necessary or if the filtration along with plants are doing a good job of keeping the tank clean. Some enthusiasts also purchase a tank cleaning siphon. This works like an underwater vacuum cleaner. It will allow you to remove old food and waste at the bottom of the tank, and so lower ammonia levels.

Make sure that the water you are changing is the same temperature as the old water. It can be deadly to shock your betta with highly varying temperatures. Monitor your thermometer and if necessary, use a water heater.

The road to my heart is paved with bubbles.

-Unknown-

7

FEEDING

LET'S EAT!

Feeding is usually an afterthought for most novice betta owners. The common misconception is that any fish pellets or flakes in the pet shop will be just fine. This is not the right mind set or solution. Just as proper nutrition is important for our health and well-being, the same can be said for bettas. Also, many owners find out that their betta can have feeding "*attitudes*". They can either be incredibly picky with what they eat, or devour everything in sight. A **variety** of high quality foods is key. Just as we wouldn't enjoy lasagna for every meal, a betta won't enjoy the same dry pellets every day. While they probably aren't as taste sensitive as we are, the same daily meal won't provide them with the nutrients they need to live a long life.

Just as we looked at bettas history and origins to

provide optimal housing, we can do the same for their feeding.

What do they eat in the wild?

In the rice paddies and small streams where they reigned supreme, bettas would feast on flying insects that would float on top of the water. This along with eggs (of the insects), larvae, worms, the occasional smaller fish, and some vegetation would be their primary source of food. This makes them primarily carnivores or more specifically, insectivores. Their environment was the most determining factor for their diet. At times, choices would be limited, however, there was usually a steady diet of mosquitos, midges, and larvae available.

This style diet remains appropriate for the fluttery little betta you have at home. I find it best to provide a betta with a varied diet of the highest quality food you can afford. This does not mean the food needs to be expensive, but it should contain the appropriate ingredients. Many fish foods contain fillers, these provide no nutritional value and can cause stomach issues and bloat in your fish. Fillers are necessary in some foods as they help bind the food, however there are differences in quality. I recommend checking the ingredients and trying to keep as few fillers as possible in your bettas diet.

What to Feed Your Betta

I recommend replicating a diet similar to the food a betta would eat naturally. There are plenty of affordable options beyond pellets available at most pet shops or online. Other than pellets alone, frozen foods, gel foods, and live foods are great options.

A simple solution that provides a good amount of variety is 2-3 different food groups. This simply means picking a minimum of 2 or 3 items out of the following options: frozen foods, pellets, gel foods, and live foods.

Frozen Foods & Freeze-Dried Foods

Frozen foods are things like brine shrimp, daphnia, and blood worms that are frozen to preserve them. They are close to what bettas would eat in the wild and are a definite favorite on the menu. Frozen food will remain fresh for a long time, and it provides natural and healthy meals. Any carnivorous frozen foods should be appropriate for your betta. They can be picky however, so experiment and learn what your little guy or gal prefers eating.

Pellets

Pellets are what most people reach for immediately when they purchase fish food. There are some great pellet options out there but it is important to feed a varied diet, not only pellets. Look for a high quality option that is protein based and contains minimal filler ingredients.

Gel Foods

Gel foods are typically quite expensive but they are a high quality food source. There is usually some preparation necessary when making the food, so there will be some extra effort required. The food lasts a long time when frozen and bettas typically love it.

Live Foods

Live foods are a great option for feeding your betta. You can purchase live brine shrimp which bettas love, and I have heard of owners setting up mosquito traps intending to feed those to their fish roommates. While these live food sources are great, they can be expensive and may take a lot of effort to capture.

How Often?

Bettas vary greatly in their eating habits. How often, and how much they eat, are very situational questions. It all depends on a number of factors including their housing situation, if they have tank mates, their size, and even their personality. You will need to do some experimenting to discover your bettas eating habits. Smaller bettas may only need to eat once a day, although twice a day is common. Some may only need 1 or 2 pellets per meal, larger ones may need more. Observe your fish and try to find the balance between overfeeding and underfeeding. They should only be fed about as much as they can eat in 3 minutes. Make sure to remove all the uneaten food as it will either rot and endanger your tank, or cause your betta to overeat.

I recommend setting up feeding times, once in the morning and once at night, and simply observing their habits. If they leave a lot behind, be sure to feed less. Also, watch and make sure that you do not overfeed. They will start to look bloated and this is very unhealthy.

At times, it is healthy to fast your betta. Every now and

then, skip a day, and don't feed him or her. It allows them to clear their system and assist with their health and proper bodily functions.

Common Issues

After getting to know your betta, their eating habits are normally quite predictable. You will get to understand what they love most on the menu, and it is common for them wait near the top of the tank for you when it is feeding time. Sometimes, however, we can run into some issues. Your betta may not want to eat at all, and this could be a sign that something is wrong.

Why is my betta not eating?

The most common reason a betta stops eating is due to overfeeding. It can really be as simple your fish just being too full from all that eating in the past weeks. Be patient and see if your betta reacts differently to the food the next day. As I mentioned before, it is great to give your fish a day off from eating once in a while. It's helpful to schedule a fasting day once every week.

It may also be because you are not feeding with enough variety. If you reach for the same frozen brine shrimp every time, your little girl or guy may just not be in the mood or hungry enough. These tropical fish need varying foods to give them all the nutrition they need.

If a betta is still not eating after these steps, observe him or her very closely. Inspect their body, scales, and fins for any signs of infections, scratches, or patches. It could be that your fish is suffering from an illness and this is causing the lack of appetite. I will cover some of the common diseases bettas can have in chapter 9. Skip ahead for more in-depth information.

It is always good to test water quality. Your betta may just not be feeling comfortable in the water he or she is in. Test the water for nitrates and ammonia and be sure to perform a water change if these elements are strong in the tank. These steps should help fix any eating disorders and have your fish back to feasting again in no time.

To everyone else I'm nothing special,
but to my fish I am the god of the
flakes...

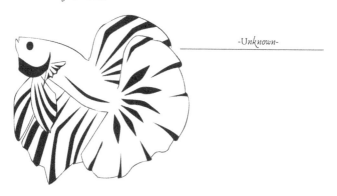

-Unknown-

8

COMPATIBILITY

BETWEEN BETTAS, SORORITIES, & OTHER FISH

As you watch your betta flutter around its tank, its normal for a thought to creep into your head.

Isn't my little guy or girl lonely in there? Won't he or she be happier with another roomie?

These are natural feelings that come from a great place. I mean, we are creatures that crave companionship. A strong social life is critical to our happiness. It's easy to set these same expectations on our bettas. Also, an active tank full of bright beautiful fish is a glorious sight. It sounds like a win-win situation. Your betta gets some companions, and you get more beautiful fish to take care of and admire. While it is possible for a betta to have tank mates, it's not a necessity, and they think of the situation very differently.

Bettas are highly territorial and are most at peace and happiest when they are in solitude. They are not schooling fish and do not pair with a mate. They just love being in their own space. Only when a male and female mate there is quick interaction. After breeding they continue on their separate ways. They have no natural desire to hang out with others, as they are simply happy "loners".

Although they are perfectly happy by themselves, it does not mean that they have to live in solitude. If you would like to add some other fish or creatures to the tank, it is definitely possible. In most cases however, it is more for the joy of the owner, rather than the betta needing tank mates.

Keeping bettas with other bettas

This is a challenge, however, it is possible.

Male bettas are the most territorial and aggressive. If you have a male, you probably won't be able to keep another betta in the same tank. If he spots another betta or another fish that looks like one, he will likely attack. Keeping a male and a female together is also unlikely to succeed. As I mentioned before, they do not bond as pairs and will only come together when it's time to mate. After the act, they will need to be separated. Some enthusiasts purchase very large tanks and then add a divider. This splits up a tank into 2 or more sections and allows them to have more than one betta in a tank. The divider is typically dark so the fish are not aware that they are sharing a home.

The only way to have multiple bettas knowingly share a tank is by creating what is called a *sorority*. A sorority is a group of female bettas sharing one tank. They are difficult to set up and you will need an appropriately sized aquarium. The ladies will organize in a manner where there is a pecking order. Once this is established, there should be peace in the sorority. They will not move around as a unit, but instead "claim" separate areas in the tank to hang out. Later on in the chapter I will go into more details about how to potentially set up a sorority.

Before I continue, I must issue a word of warning and some things to consider. Placing bettas together in one tank is very challenging and it can put a lot of stress on the fish. This stress impacts how long, and how well they live. While wild bettas do run into each other and interact, they have plenty of space to leave and continue their lives in solitude. A 10, 20-gallon tank or more simply does not replicate this well enough. There may not be a lot of aggression in the tank, but the constant stress the fish are under greatly impacts their health. It is common for bettas in sororities to get sick or have a much shorter lifespan. Even if you do not witness aggression in the tank, there are many factors at play. Please consider these health implications before attempting to set up a sorority.

Keeping Bettas With Other Creatures and Fish

There are plenty of other fish and aquatic creatures that can share a home with a betta. It is all about picking the right roommates. The first thing to consider is that they cannot be similar in appearance to a betta. Most other ornamental fish with big flowing tails or fins will just end up being a target for attacks. Fish that are too small also aren't a good option as your betta might think of them as a meal. On that same train of thought is adding fish that may think of your betta as a delicious meal. Those are obviously not the best additions to the tank.

Now that we considered these physical traits, the next step is recognizing the fact that the roommates will need to all have similar needs. Since they will share the same environment, they also need to feel at home in warm, calm water. It is important that they also enjoy some vegetation, the amount of water in the tank, and the water quality. A bettas tank mate won't need to have the same diet, as you will provide ample and the correct food for all the inhabitants. The following are some great traits to look for when considering a betta roomie:

- Non aggressive species.
- Enjoys warm water temperatures (76-82°F).
- Likes peaceful water with no strong currents.
- Bottom dwellers (fish or creatures that prefer to remain at the bottom of a tank).

If a potential roommate has these qualities, they might be a great addition to your tank. It is important to remember that tank size plays an important role in all of this working. There needs to be enough space in the tank for everyone and there needs to be enough vegetation, so if someone needs a break they can be by themselves. Also, bettas have unique personalities. Some are more open to having tank mates than others. You should prepare yourself for the fact that your betta may just not want anyone else in their tank. You might set up a tank perfectly to house a community of fish, but at the end of the day, your betta still might not be accepting of the situation. It is important not to force the matter, as it can be stressful on all the fish.

Here is a small starter list of fish and creatures that can

be great additions to a tank (These fish need at least 10-20 gallon tanks or more):

- Corydora
- Clown Pleco
- Cherry Shrimp or Ghost Shrimp
- Ember Tetra
- Guppies
- Harlequin Rasbora
- Kuhli Loach
- Otocinclus
- Zebra Snail

Sororities

When it comes to sororities, there is usually no in-between... They are either a great success story, or a massive failure. It takes a lot more work than simply placing a group of females in a tank together. While there are never any guarantees when it comes to grouping these loners together, below I summarized how to increase your chances for success.

5 Females or More...

There need to be at least 5 ladies present when you are

setting up a sorority. Having fewer means that the most dominant individuals will attack the weakest. Having at least 5 will disperse aggression, and no individual will be the weakest that gets constantly targeted and singled out.

*If you notice that some of your bettas are developing a black line running along their body, it is a sign that they are highly stressed. You may not see any aggression in the tank, but their body shows they cannot handle being in the group. Remove the fish and place her in a separate tank.

If at all possible, it is best to pick young females for a sorority. It is more likely for them to be open to having tank mates. More mature females have probably lived their entire lives in solitude. They will react more aggressively to suddenly having to share space with other bettas. Younger females might adapt to being in a community environment. It is much more difficult to distinguish between a male and female betta when they are young. Make sure you really have a group of females swimming around the tank and don't have a single male sprinkled out there as well.

The Tank

It is important to provide all the females with adequate

space within the tank. In my opinion, the tank needs to be a minimum of 15 gallons (57 L). This will help keep the situation peaceful as they can all have a bit of separation from one another. It is also best for the tank to be wider (or longer) rather than taller. Bettas enjoy coming up to the top of the tank. So the more space up there for everyone, the better.

I recommend for you to include as many plants and hiding spots as possible. It is best for sight-lines to be broken. This way each individual doesn't feel the stress of having multiple eyes on them at all times. The more plants there are, the better. It will prevent chases from happening and the ladies can claim their own hiding spots and territories.

Just like you need a cover for your tank when have just one betta, you definitely need one for a sorority. If one of the females feels uncomfortable, she may look to jump. Having a cover over the tank prevents her from jumping out. Keep a close eye on the group and if they are not getting along, find a solution where you can keep everyone separate.

Water quality in a sorority is of the utmost importance. The females can be under a lot of stress so their immune system won't be at the highest level. It is important to regularly check the condition of the tanks water and to perform regular water changes. Also, sickness can spread quickly in community tanks. Monitor water parameters and fish behavior carefully.

Follow the guidelines mentioned above to have the best chance at successfully starting a sorority. Remember, some bettas simply won't want to share a tank... and that's okay. Don't force the situation, stay positive and make the best of it. You can purchase more tanks and/or add dividers. You also have the chance of spreading the joy of fish keeping and giving an amazing gift to a loved one who is interested in owning a betta. There is always a solution.

My fish is BETTA then yours!

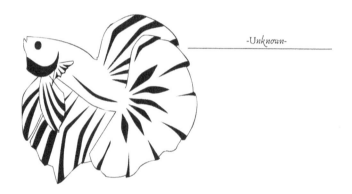

-Unknown-

9

DISEASES & TREATMENTS

If you take good care of a betta, disease rarely occurs. If you follow all the steps laid out in this book, everything should be fine. Sometimes, however, things are just out of our control. Our beautiful betta friends can get sick. Although they are some of the most durable pets available, they are still susceptible to a variety of illnesses. In these rare cases, it is great to have the information laid out in this chapter available to you. I will cover some of the more common illnesses or problems you can face when caring for your betta.

I did my best to cover many of the problems you may face, however; it is important to continue to do your own research for your specific issue. Some issues may require much more work which goes beyond the scope of this book. Please visit a licensed professional or veterinarian if you are ever unsure about how to treat your fish. Treatments of illnesses should be taken seriously and dealt with proper diligence.

What Causes Sickness

The leading cause for bettas to get sick lies in their environment. It can be water quality, not enough space, stress from tank mates, or a variety of other things... that all lead back to environment. It is best to take a preventative stance and make sure everything is a-okay in their home and with their surroundings. This will reduce the chance that your betta will ever get sick.

Review everything we covered in chapter 6 and make sure your betta has enough space and a comfortable home. Also, remember to perform frequent water quality tests. Water can appear to be nice and clean to the naked eye, but in reality it can contain high doses of things like chlorine, ammonia, or nitrate which can be deadly for bettas.

Stress also shouldn't be an underestimated factor in the wellbeing of your betta. Stress can cause a betta to stop eating, hide, and damage their immune system. This allows for infections or bacteria to come in and make a betta sick. Make sure they are perfectly happy in their home and don't force any tank mates or items in their environment that they don't respond well to.

Some enthusiasts add elements to their tank that can support the immune system of their fish. Items like Indian almond leaves, peat moss pellets, and tannins are said to assist recovery and help prevent illness. Certain water conditioners available in fish/pet shops can periodically also be added to a tank. They help promote good health and with skin repair. Talk with a store specialist to pick a great conditioner brand that can be added any time there are potential signs of illness.

How to Tell a Betta is Sick

Over time, you will really get to know your little guy or girl. You will come to distinguish normal behavior from unusual behavior. If you notice any strange activity, trust your instincts and check if anything is wrong in the tank. Inspect your bettas body and fins for any signs of ailments or symptoms. The earlier you can identify that something is wrong, the greater the chance for treatment. Here are some tell-tale signs that your betta is not feeling 100%:

- Strange swimming behavior - A betta will swim against items in the tank as if he or she wants to rub something off of their body. They may also stay at the bottom of the tank or in a corner.

- They are inactive and do not eat.
- A swollen belly, or a swelling body. Also look for swelling in their eyes.
- Their color is less vibrant and appears faded.
- Their scales are raised.
- Their gills are puffy or have reddened.
- See if their fins look to be clumped together and simply don't look healthy.
- They have lumps, spots, or growth on their body.

As I mentioned above, early detection is critical. If you notice anything is wrong, take action immediately. Test the water and move the betta to a tank where you are sure the water quality is great.

Ways to Approach Treatment

There are two main ways to treat common diseases. The first approach is a more "natural" one. It allows for the natural healing process to take place and revolves around performing increased water changes with the addition of salt treatments. Just cleaning the environment and adding some aquarium salt will help cure most ailments.

The other way to approach treatment is with the help of medication. Some illnesses require a betta to "take" medication. This can be harsh on a fish's organs but may be the only way to cure the disease.

Most Common Diseases

Here is a list of some of the most common diseases a betta might contract. I will describe the symptoms of the disease along with some treatment tips and options. Remember, some things may require help from a specialist. If you feel lost, it is best to meet with a veterinarian.

Fungal Infections & Bacterial Infections

Fungal and bacterial infections are highly contagious and typically grow on bettas. It is more likely for one of these infections to occur because of another issue like an injury or a weakened immune system.

Symptoms:

A betta suffering from these infections will have patches

or sores on their body. These patches can be white or red and may have a cottony appearance. Their coloring will be more pale and their fins will be clamped. They will be very inactive and potentially won't eat.

Treatment:

Some enthusiasts try to lower the water temperature below a bettas liking (Below 75°F). This is because funguses and bacteria thrive in the warm waters just as bettas do. Perform daily water changes and add a salt treatment (1 teaspoon of aquarium salt per gallon). If you see no improvement after 10 days or the infections spread, quickly add medication. The following items can help: Sulfa, Erythromycin, Tetracycline, along with various "fungus eliminators".

Tail Rot/Fin Rot and Fin Biting

Tail rot or fin rot is a bacterial infection that weakens fins. Fins will appear to "melt" away, and if not treated quickly can cause a lot of damage.

Symptoms:

At first your betta may not behave any different, but you will notice their fins and/or tail are getting shorter. They start having the appearance that their fins are melting, dissolving, or falling apart. This disease can advance quickly and can affect the body as well. If the rot spreads to the body, it will be hard to reverse the effects of the disease. If caught early enough, the damage to the fins or tail can be reversed.

Treatment:

Perform 100% daily water changes. Also, add aquarium salt to the tank (1 tsp/gal). I recommend adding "stress coat" to help repair damaged tissue in the fins and/or tail. If after 4 days there is no improvement increase the amount of aquarium salt to 2 teaspoons per gallon. Don't perform salt treatments for longer than 8-10 days.

Adding anti bacterial medication to your tank can also help the healing process, if aquarium salt and daily water changes don't show improvement. Use a combination of Tetracycline and Fungus Eliminator to get rid of the bacterial infection fully. Continue with treatment until the fins and tail stop receding and show growth. Stay at it, as it can take up to 4 weeks to work.

Fin biting differs greatly from fin rot. With fin biting, a betta will bite chunks off of their own tail. You will see that chunks are missing from their fin and they will look ragged. The cuts in the fins will be clean and show no discoloring. You may notice that your betta is swimming in tight circles similar to a dog chasing its tail.

There could be several reasons for fin biting so it will be worth trying out several things to see if it helps stop the behavior. They may be bored or frustrated with something in their environment. Make sure they are in an appropriately sized tank, he or she may need more space. Another option is to move things around in the tank, this may spark some curiosity and keep him or her busy exploring. Also consider adding more variety to their diet. Test some different things and see if the behavior changes. Also, it is important to frequently change their water. Their wounds can get infected more easily if they are swimming around in unhealthy water.

Dropsy

This is an internal (bacterial) infection that can come from improper housing or malnutrition. The earlier you can identify this disease the better as it can quickly become fatal.

Symptoms:

A betta will appear blown up and bloated. It will be so puffed up that their scales raise up from all the pressure. Earliest symptoms include swelling in their eyes and a gray belly. Their fins may also appear clamped and they will be very inactive.

Treatment:

It is important to treat this disease as early as possible. I recommend anti-fungal/parasite pellets along with Tetracycline, Erythromycin, or Metronidazole.

Ick

Ick is very contagious and is a parasitic infection that shows itself clearly by covering a betta with white spots.

Symptoms:

A betta with Ick will have lots of white spots all over their body and even their eyes. They may try to rub their body against items in the tank to get rid of the parasites. Their fins can start to clamp and they may not eat very much.

Treatment:

Ick is sensitive to temperature. Many enthusiasts will perform a water change and increase the temperature of the tank to around 85°F. The next step is to try treatment with aquarium salt (1 teaspoon per gallon). Water changes need to happen daily as parasites will fall off of your Betta but will still try to multiply in the water. If aquarium salt treatments don't work, try treatment with anti-parasite medication or specialized Ick treatments.

Popeye

Popeye causes the eyes of a betta to swell up. It can happen to a single eye or both. It is unlikely to kill a betta, but it can cause blindness or losing an eye.

Symptoms:

A bettas eyes or eye will swell, and can pop out of the socket.

Treatment:

This can be a challenging disease to cure. I recommend daily water changes along with a "general cure", Tetracycline, or a Fungus cure. In some cases it may be necessary to use antibiotics.

Velvet

Velvet is often called the "*gold dust disease*". It is an infection that shows a rust or gold colored dust on a bettas body.

Symptoms:

It looks like there is gold-ish dust covering a bettas body. It can be more easily seen by shining a flashlight on the betta. They may also display behavior of rubbing against items in the tank to get rid of the "dust". Their fins will also appear to be clamped and they won't eat.

Treatment:

Velvet requires the same treatment steps as Ick. Raise the temperature of the tank and use anti-parasite medication.

Inflamed Gills

Gills will swell up with this disease and prevent a betta from breathing properly.

Symptoms:

One gill or both cannot close all the way. It will appear red and simply, not close. A betta will gasp to breathe properly.

Treatment:

This disease may be caused by poor water quality. It can be that your betta has ammonia or nitrate poisoning. Water changes along with some aquarium salt or stress coat can already clear this problem up quickly. If the disease came from a bacterial infection, try treatment with Tetracycline, Sulfa, or Maracyn.

We just covered a wide variety of ailments a betta can suffer from. Most things can be treated relatively well with just water changes along with aquarium salt. Still, it's helpful to have some supplies at home quickly in reach to help with treatment. That brings us to the following...

A First Aid Kit

It may sound a bit over the top, but you cannot deny that it is helpful to have some simple things at home in case anything goes wrong. Below is a list of useful items to have for your bettas first aid kit:

- An extra 1 gallon or more container. This extra tank is very useful if you need to treat a sick betta. You can more easily perform water changes in this small tank and add treatment.
- Aquarium Salt. This is a go to treatment for aquariumists. It is great for general health and really helps with minor treatments.

- <u>Multipurpose Treatments</u>. For mild diseases, these provide a great boost for your betta.
- <u>Antibiotic Treatments</u>. Items like Tetracycline, Ampicillin, and Kanamycin.
- <u>Fungus Cures</u>. Anti-fungal treatments like a Fungus Eliminator, Sulfa, and Erythromycin.

You BETTA believe it!

-Unknown-

WHAT'S NEXT...

TIPS, FACTS & TRICKS

We covered a wide variety of topics throughout this book so far... from the history of this gorgeous fish to a variety of care aspects. You are well on your way to becoming a betta fish expert! With the knowledge you have accumulated so far, your betta will be sure to have a very healthy and happy life.

I wanted to add one more chapter to this book that will give you some closing tips and tricks. Although it takes a little bit of work, owning a betta is an amazing and very rewarding experience. I have created a simple planner below that will help you keep up with some of the more routine tasks required.

Daily Activities:

Check on the Little Guy or Girl
Observe their body and fins for any damage or signs of illnesses. Also check their behavior to see if they are acting strange or swimming in a weird way.

Feeding Time
Follow your feeding schedule. Appropriately feed your betta once or twice a day. (Schedule in a break day once a week or, once every other week.)

Check the Tank Temperature
Make sure it's a nice and cozy temperature in the tank. (76-82°F or 24-27°C)

Socialize
Enjoy owning a betta fish! Just admire their beauty, play with them, or try teaching them a trick.

Weekly Activities:

Check One, Two!
Make sure everything is functioning in the tank. Check on the heater, filter, lights, or anything else you may have in the tank and see if it is working properly.

Test the Water
Test the water quality with some strips, or head to your local fish or pet shop as many of them perform free water tests for you.

Do a Water Change
Replace around 25% of the water in your tank.

Monthly Activities:

Perform a More Thorough Cleaning
The tank may have built up some excess algae or other items.
Clean the filters and other items you may have in the tank.

Bigger Water Change
Depending on the size of your tank, you may want
to replace 60% to 100% of the water.

Betta Tips & Facts

Buy A BIG Tank

A regret I hear often from betta enthusiasts is that they didn't buy a bigger aquarium right away. Many of the tanks that are marketed for betta fish, specifically, are far too small. These environments are damaging for a betta and can lead to a much shorter lifespan. Many of us fall in love with the hobby and want to expand on their tank. You will want to add elements to the environment, and it is best to have a large tank for this. You may want some additional tank mates for your betta before you know it. Having a large tank from the start makes this a much simpler transition.

Bettas Can Change Colors

Betta fish can and usually will change their color. It is common for a betta to have much brighter and deeper colors after he or she is moved out of a pet shop and in your own properly sized tank. Simply being in a healthier environment will allow their personalities and colors to pop.

It is also common for a betta to take on a paler look when they are sick. You will be able to tell quickly they are not feeling their best. Look for any other clear symptoms and have a look through Chapter 9 in this book to help with treatment.

Some betta also have the "marble" coloration to them. These guys and girls are capable of changing their colors in just a few weeks. There is a mutation in their genes that allows them to move different chromosomes. This results in the changing of their colors and patterns.

Don't rush the process of placing a Betta in a new tank (Cycling)

Before placing any fish in a new tank, it is important to "cycle" the tank first. Cycling is the process of forming friendly bacterial colonies in a new tank. This allows the fish to have a healthy environment to live in, without high levels of toxic ammonia and nitrates. The process can take some weeks to complete, so be patient to be sure that your fish enter the correct environment.

Breeding

The focus of this book is to give a great overview on how to properly care for a betta. Breeding betta fish goes beyond the scope of this and would require a book by itself. I still wanted to include a small section on the process and explain some details that are involved.

Betta fish make bubble nests. Bubble nests are where they "house" their babies and where a male betta protects them. A male and female will come together and a male will wrap his body around the female and "squeeze" eggs out of her. It is not always a gentle act and the female can sustain some wounds. After all the eggs are extracted, the female will leave or need to be removed, or she will eat the eggs. The male will take the eggs up to the bubble nest and protect and care for them until they become fry.

Tricks to Teach Your Betta

Betta fish can actually learn some tricks. Similar to dogs, they can be taught specific acts with food as an incentive. Below are 3 tricks you can teach your betta. Remember, do not overfeed your betta. You can practice these tricks around meal time so you won't feed too many treats throughout the day. These tricks will need to be taught over several days. Be patient and your little guy or girl will get the hang of things soon enough. You will be surprised how quickly they can get the hang of things.

· · ·

Follow the leader

This is a simple trick that some bettas already do naturally. You can see if your betta already naturally has the inclination to follow your finger or a small, tank proof stick. When you have your bettas attention lightly place your finger outside of your aquarium (don't tap or hit aggressively). Slowly move your finger around to see if your betta follows you.

You can enhance this trick with the use of a small, tank proof training stick and some treats your betta loves to eat.

- Touch the training stick in the water near your betta. Then place a little bit of the food with it.

- Move the stick to another spot in the tank, (not too far from your betta) and also place some food there... Your betta will follow the food, and the stick.

- Repeat this several times and your betta will associate the training stick with food. Every time he or she sees it, he/she will go after it because of the delicious snack.

- Over time, you will be able to move the training stick a little bit and your betta will follow it. After some days or weeks you will be able to move the stick further and further with a loyal betta patiently following your moves.

- This is the basis for training a betta. Many tricks can be expanded on, from just this simple "trick" that has your betta following you.

Hoops and Tunnels

Some enthusiasts create a water-safe hoop or a tunnel to add to their tank. They expand on the "follow the leader" trick and are able to lead their betta through this hoop or tunnel. It's quite impressive to see. This is how you can get started as well...

- Purchase or make a hoop that is safe to add to an aquarium. Make sure it is big enough for your betta to safely swim through and that it doesn't have any sharp or rough materials edges to it.

- Once your betta has mastered the "follow the leader" trick try to lead him or her through the hoop.

- It is best to start right by the by the hoop so that you won't need to first lead him or her a long distance to start with.

- This trick can be expanded on by guiding your betta through a tunnel or some other safe obstacle.

The Flying Betta

As you already know, bettas are excellent jumpers. Some enthusiasts have trained their bettas to jump up for some food.

- Stick some food loosely to the end of your training stick.

- Hold the stick very close to the surface of the water (without dipping the stick in the water).

- Stay very still, and with a little bit of patience your betta will make the leap and grab the food.

- Over time, you can increase the distance you hold the stick out of water and there you will have... "The flying Betta".

These tricks are meant to be fun, bonding experiences between owner and pet. Please do not tease your fish and be sure to reward all the tiny progressions he or she makes. Some betta will get the hang of these tricks fast and some may take a bit longer. Be patient, and you will be amazed with what these smart little guys and girls can achieve.

99% sure my soulmate is a BETTA fish...

-PBS-

THANK YOU

Owning a betta is an incredibly rewarding experience. They mesmerize viewers with their gorgeous colors and captivate with their uniquely sassy personalities.

Thank you for *diving* into this amazing hobby and for learning more about these funny guys and girls.
You are now an even *"betta"* fish owner...
(*Sorry I know that was bad, but I just had to throw that in there*)

Enjoy taking care of your fish roommate and I wish you much success and joy.

If you have a second, I would truly appreciate you leaving a short review wherever you purchased this book. Your opinion in a quick sentence or two will already help tremendously.

Thank you for your time and have an awesome time caring for your flappy friend.

Cheers,
Walter

It doesn't get any BETTA than this!

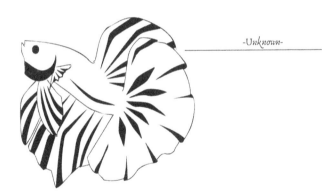

-Unknown-

RESOURCES

Besides my own knowledge and experiences, I used the following awesome sources to create this book:

Admin. "Betta Fish Care Guide." *Betta Fish World*, 4 Aug. 2019, bettafishworld.com/betta-fish-care-guide/.

Anderson, Wal. "Betta Anatomy." *The Basic Anatomy of Betta Splendens.*, watershed3.tripod.com/anatomy.html.

"Betta Bellica – Slender Betta (Betta Fasciata)." *Seriously Fish*, www.seriouslyfish.com/species/betta-bellica/.

"Betta Bellica." *International Betta Congress*, 9 June 2018, www.ibcbettas.org/about-betta-splendens/smp/species/bellica/.

"Betta Care Sheet." *Aqueon Aquarium Products: It's All*

about the Fish!, www.aqueon.com/information/care-sheets/betta.

"Betta Fish: Facts and History." *Betta Fish History and Facts*, www.bettafishcenter.com/betta-history-list.shtml.

"Betta Imbellis – Crescent Betta." *Seriously Fish*, www.seriouslyfish.com/species/betta-imbellis/.

"Betta Pugnax (Betta Bleekeri, Betta Macrophthalma)." *Seriously Fish*, www.seriouslyfish.com/species/betta-pugnax/.

Bob. "How Often to Change Betta Fish Water: How to Change Betta Fish Water." *Betta Answers*, Bob Hennessey, 30 Oct. 2019, www.bettaanswers.com/changing-betta-fish-water/.

Bryan. "Betta Fish Anatomy - Plus Male And Female Differences." *Bettafish.org*, bettafish.org/betta-fish-anatomy/.

Craig. "How Do Betta Fish Breathe In & Out Of Water." *Aquascape Addiction*, 27 Apr. 2019, www.aquascapeaddiction.com/articles/how-do-betta-fish-breathe.

"Do Betta Fish Change Color?" *Betta Source*, 29 June 2019, bettasource.com/do-betta-fish-change-color/.

Fanatic, Aqua. "Betta Anatomy." *Aqua Fanatic*, aquafanatic.blogspot.com/2011/07/betta-anatomy.html.

Fernando, Yohan. "Spawning Betta Smaragdina – the 'Emerald Betta.'" *International Betta Congress*, 27 Dec. 2017, www.ibcbettas.org/about-betta-splendens/smp/articles/emeraldbetta/.

Hamilton, B. "Betta Fish Care Guide: A One Page Care Sheet - All You Need to Know!" *Www.itsafishthing.com*, 19 Oct. 2019, www.itsafishthing.com/betta-fish-care/.

Hamilton, B. "Betta Fish Diseases, Symptoms and Treatment Guide." *Www.itsafishthing.com*, 19 Oct. 2019, www.itsafishthing.com/betta-fish-diseases/.

Hamilton, B. "How to Breed Betta Fish: Expert A to Z Guide, All You Need to Know." *Www.itsafishthing.com*, 19 Oct. 2019, www.itsafishthing.com/how-to-breed-betta-fish/.

Hamilton, B. "Types of Betta Fish – By Tail, Pattern and Color, With Photos." *Www.itsafishthing.com*, 9 Nov. 2019, www.itsafishthing.com/types-of-betta-fish/#types-of-betta-fish-by-pattern.

Hamilton, B. "What Do Betta Fish Eat? A Guide To Feeding Betta Fish." *Www.itsafishthing.com*, 9 Oct. 2019, www.itsafishthing.com/what-do-betta-fish-eat/.

"How to Help Keep Your Pet Fish Alive." *Aqueon Aquarium Products: It's All about the Fish!*, www.aqueon.com/articles/how-to-help-keep-your-pet-fish-alive.

IBC Bettas. "About Betta Splendens." *International Betta Congress*, 6 July 2018, www.ibcbettas.org/about-betta-splendens/.

Info, Betta. "Betta Fish Tail Types." *Japanesefighting-fish.org*, 22 Apr. 2018, japanesefightingfish.org/betta-fish-tail-types/.

Kathryn, Wendy. "How to Cycle a Fish Tank: Easy to Follow Step-by-Step Guide." *Www.itsafishthing.com*, 19 Oct. 2019, www.itsafishthing.com/how-to-cycle-a-fish-tank/.

Matt. "Betta Splendens – Siamese Fighting Fish (Micra-canthus Marchei)." *Seriously Fish*, www.seriouslyfish.com/species/betta-splendens/.

N/A. "Betta Fish Care." *Betta Fish Care*, home.adelphi.edu/~ve21375/Betta%20Fish%20Care.html.

N/A. "How Can I Play with My Betta Fish." *Aqueon*, 2017, www.aqueon.com/articles/how-can-i-play-with-my-betta-fish.

Short, Adam. "Betta Behavior - Male and Female Betta Fish." *Female Betta Fish Characteristics and Male Betta Fish Behavior*, 2013, www.bettafishcenter.com/Betta-Behavior.shtml.

Short, Adam. "Betta Fish Aquarium Behavior." *Betta*

Fish Aquarium Behavior, 14 June 2013, www.bettafishcenter.com/betta-aquarium-behavior.shtml.

Short, Adam. "Betta Fish History – From Then Until Now." *Betta Fish Center*, 2013, www.bettafishcenter.com/betta-fish-history-then-now.shtml.

Short, Adam. "Betta Fish – All the Colors of the Rainbow." *Betta Fish - All the Colors of the Rainbow*, www.bettafishcenter.com/betta-colors-rainbow.shtml.

Short, Adam. "Betta Types – Physical Appearances." *Types of Bettas*, www.bettafishcenter.com/Betta-Types.shtml.

Tetra Fish. "Betta - Betta Splendens." *Tetra*, www.tetrafish.com/fish-type-landing/betta.aspx.

Tricks, Spartan's, director. *5 Easy Tricks to Teach Your Betta Fish First. YouTube*, YouTube, 13 Sept. 2018, www.youtube.com/watch?v=4flOnHwSslc.

Trr. "How to Keep Your Aquarium Fish Healthy - the 10 Top Tips." *The Spruce Pets*, The Spruce Pets, 27 Feb. 2018, www.thesprucepets.com/fish-health-1381302.